Great Things Come to Those Who ~~Wait~~

Take Action!

D0763015

Kevin Mullens

FZM Publishing

PO Box 3707

Hickory, NC 28603

Copyright 2015

By Kevin Mullens

All Scriptures, unless indicated, are taken from the King James Version (KJV).

Scripture quotations marked NIV are taken from the New International Version.

Scripture quotations marked NLT are taken from the New Living Translation.

ISBN

978-0-9891997-5-9

Printed in the United States of America

Table of Content

Introduction 7

You are What You Consistently Do 17

Book of Acts: Taking ACTSion 27

The Consequences of Counterproductive Chatter 37

Battle is the Doorway to Living in the Promise Land 47

The Wisdom of Ants 67

Great Things Come to Those Who **TAKE ACTION** 83

Final Thoughts: Paying the Price 93

Kevin Mullens

Introduction

So often we dream or envision what things could be like, IF. If only we had more time, more education, more energy, more... more... more! The truth is that change will never happen until we change. We are all aware that if we are to earn more, then we must become more. Wisdom has always been the key that unlocks a season of overflow, abundance, and divine favor. But all of the wisdom in the world won't do us any good if we don't back it up with a plan of massive, immediate action. As the scripture says, the harvest is ready but the laborers are few (Matthew 9:37). God's principles are sovereign and always produce a great harvest when they are applied with unwavering faith, but the principles of Christ only bring forth increase when they are applied through action. You can say you desire financial freedom or even a certain girl or boy to marry but the only poof that reflects what you want, is the level of your pursuit.

I can remember the first time I ever saw my wife. I was consumed with this thing they call love at first sight. I literally walked up to her and said,

"I am going to marry you!" As you might imagine, she didn't quite feel this way, YET. We even lived in two different states, but after meeting her and watching her go to a state over 500 miles away, I knew there was only one sane thing to do. Yep, I moved to North Carolina. Even then I couldn't get her attention. I was not discouraged one bit. I had already put an image of this beautiful angel in my mind and nothing would persuade me differently. I pursued until, I am sure, it could have been considered stalking at this point. Through much effort, poems, flowers sent, and yes, even begging, I was able to finally get that first date. The rest of the story is a novel in itself, but here I am today still married to the love of my life some 25 years later.

So many people want something, but when met by opposition or rejection, they seem to lose their passion to do the things necessary to get what they truly want. I want you to stop giving up so soon. I want you to recognize that it is the voice of the enemy – the voice of fear telling you "it's just too tough" or "you're not capable..." You can silence his voice through intense focus and action. This is also the only way to know if you have truly made a decision. It's always backed up by action. I want you to read this book and let the words rekindle a fire in your soul to go forth and relentlessly pursue your dreams and desires with such determination that your dreams begin to pursue you. Many will say what they are going to do, but you are what you do; not what you say you'll do. Solomon said, **"Lazy people want much but get little, but those that work hard will prosper."** (Proverbs 13:4)

Growth doesn't just happen. You don't just become a great leader. Many books are written on leadership alone but the real measure of a leader is, ACTION. Take the case of the great Macedonian conqueror Alexander the Great. In the year 333 B.C. a young Alexander the Great was in the beginning stages of what would become his conquest of much of the known world. Knowing the Greeks affinity for omens and other supernatural portends, Alexander sought to fulfill the prophecy of the Gordian knot. The prophecy stated that the man who loosened the knot would conquer Asia. Alexander knew that if he were to fulfill the prophecy, then his armies would believe that the heaven's favored Alexander and would unflinchingly follow him in pursuit of his destiny. Upon seeing the gigantic knot and ineffectual attempts at untying the knot, Alexander stepped back and tried a different approach. He drew his sword and sliced through the knot and watched it fall loosely to the ground. The knot was destroyed after that action by Alexander, so one of two things had to be true: either the prophecy was false, or Alexander had fulfilled it.

Alexander thought outside of the box. He did not let boundaries of common thinking hinder him from the apprehension of his goal. Alexander did not view it as something that may OR may not happen for him. Alexander took ACTION! Alexander MADE IT HAPPEN! The rest, as they say, is history. Alexander's conquest led him to defeat the mighty Persian Empire, carving out his own Empire that stretched from Greece to the Hindu Kush. The question that you may find yourself asking, "How do I become an individual of ACTION? How do I apprehend my dreams?"

It's always a great start to get your thoughts focused on what you want, but that's not enough. You must align your thoughts with directed action so that thing you have focused on will be materialized. I am fully convinced that the Law of Attraction begins to work when we apply the Law of Action. I trust you will begin to see that just a little more effort in certain areas of your life will create a tipping point, so you can begin to experience momentum. We know that at 211 degrees that water is very hot, but at 212 degrees water begins to boil. Its only 1 degree but it makes all the difference in the world. I want to communicate to you very boldly that you can go succeed on purpose, and that you are the CEO of your own destiny. Yes, it will take an unusual effort, unusual focus, and unusual determination, but the result will be receiving an unusual reward. Generating unusual income so you can go pursue the things you are passionate about without financial restraint.

We are aware that we can't have a million dollar dream come true with a minimum wage work ethic. So many people have access to the same opportunities, and some make money while most just make excuses. This can be found in both your natural life and spiritual life. You will also need a millionaire mindset to attract and manifest the things in your life that you desire. You must guard your thoughts, because they lead to words and we know the power of words bring forth life or death. We literally prophesy our future by the words we declare. The creative power within us will always materialize the thoughts we give the most attention to. John 15:7 says, **"If ye abide in me, and my WORDS abide in you, ye shall ask what ye will and it shall be done unto you."** Words become actions and actions determine our future. In my book, *More Than Enough*, I discussed God's will for you to prosper in every area of your live. I put to rest this nonsense doctrine of poverty and challenge you to dream bigger, to do MORE. Be MORE. Never settle for less than what God has promised you. In this book, I am going to challenge you to not only decree positive affirmations and scriptural truths, but to

The creative power within us will always materialize the thoughts we give the most attention to.

match your vision with consistent effort so you can see what you have dreamed about become a reality. WORDS MATTER! Words backed by actions matter more!

The journey will require some discipline. There will definitely be some battles that you are going to have to fight, but you can rest assure that God has well equipped you to go the distance. The enemy is only fighting you because he has recognized your future and seeks to steal, kill, and destroy. You are stronger than you think. You are designed to do the impossible and live life more abundantly. So few will experience the Promise Land, because so many have given in to a life of mediocrity.

Don't you dare sit on your dreams and relinquish your right to have all that God has promised you. Do what others will not do, so you can have what they will never have. Maximum effort will create maximum rewards. Some can stay excited for a day or two. Others will stay excited for a month or two, but winners will stay excited until the job is done. Just raw get it done attitude that has decided to get up after every failure and keep on keeping on. Not just being in motion. Lots of people are in motion, planning what to do, doing lots of research on what to do. Motion sounds really good, but it will never produce the results you are looking for. Motion can even be exhausting and time consuming, but it's incapable of producing the desired outcome. We all go about doing things a little differently, but the entrepreneur starts with the end in mind, and because their eye is on the prize, they just succeed on purpose because they are determined to get the job done.

Imagine Jacob in the Bible whose name meant supplanter, which was deceiver. What an identity to have to live with; but Jacob desired the father's inheritance. He wanted to transform and change his future so badly that he wrestled an angel all night and refused to let the angel go until he blessed him. That relentless and unwilling to quit nature of Jacob was determined to see a change in his life. A new destiny was unfolding because he took massive immediate action. Desperation kicked in and Jacob decided in order for his circumstances to change, that he would need a change. I am telling you, I would've wrestled an angel too if that's what it was going to take for me to win the heart of that blue-eyed beauty from the Carolinas back in 1989. I was relentless, and relentless people get what they want.

Are you ready for a change? Health? Spiritual? Family? Income? Are you ready to live the life God promised you? Are you ready to take the action necessary to break all strongholds in your life to bring about the blessings of God? God is calling you to a Life Unlimited, where you push beyond the limits and barriers that have previously held you captive. It is time for you to sail away from the safe harbor of average and ordinary, and experience the ocean of extraordinary. It's like Zig Ziglar said, "You don't have to be great to start, but you have to start to be great." I pray that you get a burning desire to pursue something relentlessly, so you can see the manifestation of your ideas in action.

"For with God, NOTHING SHALL BE IMPOSSIBLE." Luke 1:37

Kevin Mullens

Chapter One

You Are What You Consistently Do

You are what you consistently do. The things you do day in and day out create your habits. Often I hear people say, time will change everything, but they are wrong. The only thing that's going to bring forth change is doing things differently. Your job, your spiritual walk, your relationships are all determined by our previous actions. Your life is the sum of your habits. How successful you are or are not is the result of habit. How in shape you are or are not is the direct result of habit. How skilled or qualified you are, in any area, is the result of habit. So, whether you're working out to get in shape or involved in a business to increase your quality of living, you are going to be right where you are right now, unless you start changing things that you do on a daily basis. This holds true especially in the world of business Most will never see the life they've dreamed about, because it requires them to become better. More qualified.

There will always be people more talented than you, but there is never a reason for anyone to outwork you. I love the quote that Tim Tebow had on his wall growing up: "Hard work beats talent when talent don't work hard." You have got to start asking yourself, "Is what I am currently doing going to get me closer to my goals?" If I keep doing what I am currently doing, will anything ever change? Brother Branham said, "What you do everyday determines what you are." Even your bank account reflects your business and money habits. Habits either serve you or they don't. They either take you toward your intended outcome or away from it. Knowing your beliefs is the key to changing habits.

Have you ever had someone say to you, "You haven't changed a bit"? This isn't a good thing! It's not a compliment! If you are learning, then you are growing. So if you are still perceived as the exact same person, it means you have not grown. Then of course, there are those who cannot stand it when you have made a decision to succeed. They will say, "You have changed." This is a great compliment because it means that you have decided to stop living your life according to their ideas of you. Change is inevitable. Your life is compiled of seasons, and these seasons are determined by our daily activity. Winning is a habit but so is losing. Whether we talk about failure or excellence, they both are the product of habit, which arrived from your actions. This is why we see history repeating itself, because our lives are reflecting what we consistently do. The highly successful have mastered doing the things daily that bring forth their desired result.

Most people love to think others just got lucky somehow, but it's just not true. They have radically enforced all things necessary in their life to bring about the things they want most. What things will you do every day to get closer to the things you have dreamed about? Will you read every day? Exercise every day? Study God's Word more consistently? Connect with influencers, doers, and difference makers? Whatever it is you have been praying for or dreaming about will begin to show up just as you envisioned.

Your behavior, your verbiage, and your posture will all be altered in such a positive way through alignment with the right activity every day to create the atmosphere in your life for favor; to bring those things to you that you have been longing for. Many of you already know what to do but knowing is not enough. People spend thousands of dollars on training materials, conferences, books and even degrees to learn how to become a successful entrepreneur but nothing ever changes until that knowledge is implemented. Put forth the effort every single day, stay focused on the end result and you will begin to realize that the great secret to tremendous success is hidden in your daily routine. Revaluate your vision. Look at all the things you do day in and day out, to see if what you are doing lines up with making your vision becomes reality.

Observe the information you are drawing your belief system from because what you believe about yourself will be apparent in your actions. Your actions and words reflect your beliefs. When you believe a certain thing about yourself, or anything, or anyone, you ACT, speak, and think accordingly. Ultimately, you are what you believe you are. If you believe you can, then you can, and if you believe you can't, then you can't. Know that your habits are the results of your beliefs. You cannot expect to permanently change a negative habit into a positive one if its underlying belief remains negative. To successfully and permanently transform your bad habits into positive ones, you must also **CHANGE YOUR BELIEFS**.

All that you are is the product of someone's teaching, whether that is parents, pastor, or circle of friends you put trust in. This is why most of what you think is not even your own thoughts. Everything that you habitually do, say, or think today, started off as a single action or thought, which was repeated often enough until it was passed down to your subconscious mind where it formed a habit. This is why Solomon said, as a man *"... thinketh in his heart, so is he"* (Proverbs 23:7). That's the subconscious realm. All habits reside at the level of your subconscious mind, where you no longer have to consciously think about them. Therefore, changing habits must involve programming and re-programming your unwanted negative beliefs at the subconscious level. You must always remember that thought becomes words. and your words become actions. Your actions become habits, which become your character, and that character becomes your DESTINY.

Make a decision to develop your skills and conquer the areas of your life that are keeping you stuck at average and ordinary. The Infinite One that lives within you is waiting on you to allow His power to come forth and boldly take what is rightfully yours by a divine promise. You are predestinated for greatness. Let go of past mistakes and failures and realize that you are the architect of your future. ONLY BELIVE, ALL THINGS ARE POSSIBLE. Whatever you believe is what you say, whatever you say becomes your actions, and your actions determine who you are. <u>You will never attract what you want, but you will always attract what you are.</u>

Here are some things I want you to do that will help keep you focused and responsible for your success in life. Do not merely accept "whatever happens will happen;" you make things happen. Start moving away from saying, "I want to make this happen, to saying; I AM going to make this happen." You will soon find out that the so-called chosen ones aren't lucky at all. Before they were ever successful they chose themselves. CHOOSE YOU!

1. **Put God first:** Proverbs 3:6 (Living Bible) *"In everything you do PUT GODFIRST and He will direct and crown your life with success."*

2. **Family:** This can be immediate or extended family, but have family to help keep you grounded. Family can also be a huge motivating factor that keeps you going.

3. **Have a vision board:** This board serves a greater purpose when you make it with your loved ones. Get them involved so they understand your relentless pursuit when sacrifices must be made. Cut out pictures of the things you want and don't hold back. DREAM BIG! Make sure your vision board is filled with all of the pictures that represent what you want so when you see it every day it reminds you of what you and your family desires.

4. **Find a mentor:** A mentor becomes a prophecy of your future so choose, even pursue if needed, someone that can give you the wisdom necessary to get you to your

desired destination. The information you need is hidden in a mentor.

5. **Take ownership of your future:** Make sure you measure everything. Keep a journal on how you are coming along with your goals. Figure out what works and what doesn't work. Have an unusual determination. FOCUS!

While we know that consistency is the Key to becoming great at anything. It's also the hardest to master because of all the distractions we encounter in our daily life. This is why I tell my leaders to cast their vision daily because people leak vision fast. Life gets in the way, and it's so easy to lose motivation and focus, much less remain consistent. Consistent actions require consistent thinking, specifically the consistent thought that you are and will remain consistent. Don't let the temporary illusions of depression, anxiety or failure keep you from executing what you need to do every day. JUST DO IT! You owe it to your dreams to push through the easy to make excuses and stay in that training mode or boot camp mindset. The mindset that demands more out of you every single day, than you ever would yourself. Learn to master the art of consistency, and you will find that can do anything or be anything you want.

"The most practical, beautiful, workable philosophy in the world won't work – if you won't." - Zig Ziglar

Kevin Mullens

Chapter Two

Book of Acts: Taking ACTSion

This is one of my favorite books in the New Testament. Many scholars call this book, the Acts of the Apostles. We must give attention to the placing of this book as it comes directly after the four gospels, which were the framework of this incredible book. In those gospels we are given many promises of what kind of power and authority the believer would have after the resurrection. We start in Acts the first chapter telling the early church that they would receive power after the Holy Ghost is come upon you. I often quote Ephesians 3:20, *"Now to Him who is able to do exceedingly, abundantly, above all that we ask or think, according to the POWER that works in US."* It is easy for people to get excited when I quote this scripture about the exceeding and abundant aspect, but the true revelation is in knowing that the POWER is IN US. Not your power but the power of the Omnipotent One.

We see God pouring out the Pentecostal blessing in Acts chapter two. I'm not talking about Pentecost as an organization but PENTECOST the experience; proving that anyone that has a genuine experience with Christ begins to ACT different. John 14 gives the church hope that although the physical body of Jesus Christ was to soon be gone, we would not be left comfortless. Promise after promise about Christ now living within and proof of His life within you would be through our ACTSions.

This tremendous book of Acts is about the ordinary doing the extraordinary. It definitely gives many accounts about the exploits demonstrated in the early church and how the supernatural was often on the scene doing signs and wonders. I am not saying that raising the dead or healing the sick is the only way to tell if God is on the scene working in the body of Christ. But our ACTSions will declare what we believe and the fruit will always bear witness. The writer of the

Word lives within the heart of every believer waiting to manifest His promises, so it is not enough to just say we believe or to rehearse scripture, but through our ACTSions we live our faith out loud. If there were to ever be another book of Acts written then it would produce the same anointing and the same evidence. One might think that the church no longer has the authority that it once had but HIS WORD is still the same. He is still the same yesterday, today and forever, but it's our faith in ACTSion that goes out and manifests the things we are declaring. That feels good so let me say that one more time, it's your FAITH IN ACTSion. If God ever acted in a certain way one time then He is obligated to act that way again. So when your faith moves into ACTSion, it moves God into ACTSion. What He did for Moses, Noah, Daniel, Job, Paul, and many more... He will do the same thing for you.

An area most people fail to see is what is required of us to see the principles of wealth or increase show up in full force. Yes, salvation is free. You need only to repent and ask Christ into your life, and there is no works necessary to receive His grace other than believe. However, walking in wealth or abundance requires not only a change in our mindset but our belief must bring forth an action that brings that thought into reality. Could God just put one million dollars into your bank account? Yes. Will He? Probably not, as He Himself is bound to a set of laws that were sovereignly put in place by Him. Like the Law of Sowing and Reaping. You can't sow corn and expect gold. It's not going to happen. You can recite affirmations and scripture until you are blue in the face but until you apply these principles in the right areas, you will see nothing change.

Naaman was told to go bathe in the river Jordan seven times to receive healing of his leprosy. The promise of God required something from Naaman. Had he only dipped six times he would not have received his healing. Obedience is KEY. Joshua was told that he would see the walls of Jericho fall and victory would be granted, but Joshua and the children of Israel were required to march around Jericho in order for the promise to come to pass. You are going to be required to do some things in order for these Kingdom Principles to manifest an abundant harvest in your life.

Toting a Bible won't make you a Christian no more than wearing a cowboy hat will make you a real cowboy. ACTSion will always be the foundation to any accomplishment or success. ASK and it shall be given. SEEK and you shall find. KNOCK and it shall be opened. All of these are verbs!!! If you sow sparingly then you will reap sparingly. There are so many promises to speak over our health, finances and family, but all of these promises require ACTSion. You might say, oh but I just believe them. Faith is a conviction expressed in a choice. It starts with belief, but if this belief does not lead to obedience and action, it is not yet faith. Your belief does not become true faith until you act upon it in obedience. Faith is belief in action. Read Hebrews 11 about the heroes of Faith, and you will see Faith acting in spite of the circumstances. That's why it's impossible to please God without faith.

Your belief does not become true faith until you act upon it in obedience.

Can you imagine when Abraham was given the promise that wherever the soles of his feet trod that it represented ownership and Abraham staying inside of his tent? Abraham would've never possessed the gate of the enemy without taking ACTSion. There will never be a convenient time to confront the things in your life that need changed. As Paul Orberson would say, "Yes, God feeds the little birds, but He doesn't open their mouths and cram worms down their throats." Paul loved to also state that it was Noah that saved Noah. We know that Jehovah gave Noah the blueprint to build the Ark and warned him of the judgment that was about to come, but it was Noah that had to actually build the Ark. This blueprint called the Bible has a formula for every situation. Most self-help books that all millionaires refer back to are filled with biblical principles. Maybe they are conveyed in a different light but the message is the same. We as spirit filled believers have the ability to see God's Favor accelerate and shift our life into maximum overflow when we apply these principles with unwavering faith.

Many today have embarked on a journey in network marketing to go participate in a global economy and create residual income. It's the smartest thing anyone can do for personal development and potential life changing income. But as you might imagine when things don't go according to plan it becomes easy to quit or make excuses. I am often asked if MLM works and I always say it works if you will work. No matter how perfect the product is or the compensation is, NONE of this will win for you. If the numbers don't change then nothing changes. You have to be able to look yourself in the mirror and be very honest with yourself about your level of activity, whether it is real estate, fishing, recruiting, or building teams. Those that are constantly doing a little more and live life going the extra mile, where so few are willing to go, will always find more wins than losses. Quit looking for the secret. Bill Britt who made multi- millions in direct sales said, "There is no secret. I simply showed the plan to 1,200 people. 900 said, NO, and only 300 signed up. Out of those 300, only 85 did anything at all. Out of those 85 only 35 were serious, and out of those 35, 11 made me a millionaire." So, the secret power of the wealthy is as simple as laser-like focus and the ability to just PRESS ON. ACTSion, ACTSion, ACTSion.

When I made a decision to go win financially, I knew I had no free time, but I made the time. I had no idea what to do, but I knew watching videos or reading books would never grow my business if I didn't put the information to work. You can't just be a hearer of the word, but you must be a doer. You will either find a way or make excuses. You know when you are giving it your all. You know when you have decided you want something and that you're really going to go for it. I feel like Jeremiah when he said it felt like fire shut up in his bones. There is a force that seems to push you toward your desired destiny once you back up your dream with ACTSion. If you only do things when you feel like doing them, then you are never going to do anything. There is way too much at stake for you to sit by watching others go pursue their dreams while you accept your current circumstances. It's time to stop pretending you're average. God has ordained you to do great things. You are needed now more than ever. Allow your calling to also become your obsession. So many want to make it out to be a bad thing when you become obsessed about something positive and transforming, but when you are obsessed there is no obstacle to great for you to overcome.

Nothing is more powerful that your willingness to move from idea or thought to pure fueled action that will not cease until you have finished your course. Christianity is ACTSion. Leadership is ACTSion, and Faith is ACTSion.

The book of Acts was about a church on fire. Acts 17 talks about a group that turned the world upside down. Go forth and be a fire starter. Unbridle your inner self that dreams of amazingly big things. Unleash that part of you that is fearless and has been waiting on you to come alive, and go live life unlimited. Fire starters don't look at how things are but see clearly how things can be. They are the spark that cast vision and builds a bridge for others to see things as they do. Fire starters live a purpose filled life that is driven by a passion to infect others with the boldness to unbridle and unleash their God given destiny. Be a one man movement that moves so intently that it moves you away from lazy people and draws towards you people of like mind, faith, and vision that want some of the same things you do. You don't need a majority to create change. A few Holy Ghost filled believers in one mind and one accord packs enough power to move mountains and do the impossible. So put your foot down and say, NO MORE to mediocrity, self-sabotage, and complacency. Your destiny to change the world one life at a time is waiting on you. As Joan of Arc said, "I am not afraid; I was born to do this."

May I say to you … YOU WERE BORN TO DO THIS!!!

"Rise up; this matter is in your hands. We will support you, so take courage and do it." Ezra 10:4

Chapter Three

The Consequences of Counterproductive Chatter

"In hard work there is always profit, but too much chattering leads to poverty." Proverbs 14:23

In a world filled with plenty of distractions, it is easy to get lost in conversation that has no value. We are already aware that we must be cautious of whose voice we allow to influence our lives, but often we submit ourselves to repetitive chatter that consumes our time. This is why all of us are guilty of putting off things that we know we need to do, or at one point wanted to do. One of the ways our enemy keeps us from achieving the extraordinary is the Art of Distraction. It's hard sometimes to distinguish what exactly it is that's got us bogged down, but we can start by eliminating or restricting things that won't get us any closer to our desired destiny. My first suggestion is turning off the TV! Yes, I know how angry you already are for me merely suggesting such an awful thing, but did you know the average American watches more than 4 hours of television every day? Over a lifespan of 65 years, that's 9 years glued to a TV. TURN OFF THE TV!!! Get unplugged from wasting hours watching most of what is purely negative and get started on living life to the fullest. Okay, okay, if you must watch your favorite show then make sure you are using a DVR to record your show so you can watch an hour program in 40 minutes. You can now get busy doing the things you once thought you had no time for. The information available today is incredible, but information overload makes things counterproductive and complicated.

Eliminate mindless internet surfing, hours worrying about who has tagged you in a picture on Facebook or if they've read your RSS feed. Much of today's electronics has done the opposite of free up time. I am so guilty of this. I literally cannot put my phone down. Yes, I conduct business globally and have the privilege of working with dedicated world changers in almost every time zone possible, but if I'm not careful, I will allow this iPhone to demand more of my time than I give to my on family. I was asked by one of my business partners how in the world I have time to author books when my schedule is already very demanding. I laughed and told her that I write my books when I am on a plane. Most domestic flights offer some restricted Wi-Fi service so I guess you could check your social sites to see what everyone is up to and engage in this constant chatter, but imagine taking a 16 hour flight from Atlanta to Nigeria. I have no internet service on this flight, and I'm not much of a sleeper so it's a great time for me to catch up on a book I needed to read or write a book. Maybe take time to pretend or imagine that you are on an international flight with no internet access. What could you accomplish without the distraction of having to check your emails or texts every 5 seconds? It's time to declutter all of the things in your mind that create so much noise that you can't seem to focus on something in order to be more effective.

I'm challenging you to go on a social media diet and limit yourself to the information that serves a purpose in your life and adds value to your aspiration and dreams.

This will help free up your time to go get in front of people on a daily basis to build your fortune on a part time basis in your home based business. Learn a new skill. Get things done around the house. Spend quality time with your family. Serve the community among many other things that will be more self-fulfilling. You will be able to look at your vision board and goals that you have set for yourself and start working on a plan of action to get things done. You don't want to be identified as the person that is, ALL TALK and NO ACTION. All bark and no bite. All hammer and no nail, or the old Texas saying, All hat and no cattle. People lose confidence in you when you have a track record of never following through or finishing. Solomon said in another place, "Whatever your hands find to do, do it with all your might" Ecclesiastes 9:10. Be sold out to doing something. Napoleon Hill talked about desire being the starting point of all achievement. Weak desires will bring weak results, but when your desires are strong enough, you will appear to possess superhuman powers to achieve.

You can see how important it is to get rid of idle, unproductive chatter and thoughts, so you can hold a desired thought long enough until action is birthed, and that thought becomes reality. You destroy any chance of success when your thoughts are consumed with negative limitations, so you must have definiteness of purpose backed up by a definite plan. ACTION is the only measure of intelligence. I love Thomas

ACTION is the only measure of intelligence.

Edison's statement, "Genius is one percent inspiration and ninety-nine percent perspiration." The great threat we face is appearing to be busy or in motion, but not taking action, or waiting on someone else to get it done for us.

Matthew 21:28-31 gives the parable of two sons. One is like a lot of people today who have good intentions. He told his father that he would go work in the field, but he didn't. It is this kind of attitude that leads to poverty as we discussed at the beginning of this chapter found in Proverbs 14:23. It's so easy to say what we are going to do, but you are not what you say you are; you are what you DO. **"They claim to know God, but by their actions they deny him"** Titus 1:16.

Do not let your dreams die within your mind and heart. Your future you will thank you for deciding to take action. Vision without action is just hallucination. Faith without works is dead, but it is also true that talk without works is dead. Give yourself the satisfaction and joy of becoming a doer. You will be surprised how easy it is to walk in FAVOR when you become addicted to getting things done. It's like the laws of wealth have noticed your arrival and begin to pursue you as hard as you pursue it. Your behavior of walking the talk and practicing what you preach will become a catalyst for others to put their faith in you. Opportunities and open doors will become more apparent as well as more lucrative. Your appreciation for living life to the absolute fullest and pushing the limits to discover life's riches lie just beyond your comfort zone. You will constantly be bombarded with reasons to quit or fade back into your old unproductive habits but hear that voice of triumph inside of you saying you can do it. You are closer than you think. You don't quit when you are tired or exhausted, but you catch that second wind and in that moment you recognize you were born to conquer. The pain and discomfort are temporary yet necessary to live in victory.

What is your pain tolerance? What will you endure to get what you want? No rain, no rainbow. No battle, no victory. President Woodrow Wilson said, "Genius is divine perseverance." P-U-S-H. Persist Until Something Happens. Coach Paul Orberson would say, "Just like dogs don't chase parked cars, people don't follow people who are stuck where they are." He would always remind us that your life and business are just like a wheelbarrow, "It stands still unless you push it." The power of ONE starts with you. What decisions will you make today that will set a series of motions in place to eventually reach the masses? Just one act followed by another.

I started with one distributor in my direct selling business and one turned into 3 and 4 and those 3 and 4 turned into 30,000 and 40,000. My wealth was only one person away, but that one person started with ME. I was in a business called network marketing, not NET-JOIN marketing. Kevin, how did you build such a successful business? I got in front of people! How often? ALL DAY, EVERYDAY. You are so much more important than you have given yourself credit. People ordained for your leadership are waiting on you to show up. When you have anchored your soul in Christ you will begin to understand that HE gave you the power (ABILITY) to get wealth. HE heals you and delivers you out of all your troubles. HE has made you the head and not the tail. HE justified you, which means you never did sin in the first place. HE gifted you to make a difference not only in the church but also in the market place.

Confront your chatter and idle talk. Contest all things in your life that are counterproductive and hindering your progress. Don't accept average and ordinary, because you are the offspring of The King of Kings. Don't live life looking in the rearview mirror always second-guessing and pondering what you could've done or should've done. The enemy's greatest tactic is to keep you doubting yourself. Our self-worth is often sold short because we remain prisoners of the past. Stop looking at where you were and start looking at where you WILL be. If God be for us, who can be against us (Romans 8:31)? You will never feel complete until you succeed. There is greatness within you; a power within you desperately waiting on you to move away from motion and empty words and go full force into MASSIVE ACTION. There comes a time when you have to move away from, "Get a vision leadership, to GETTING IT DONE leadership." That time is now. One of the greatest traits of real genuine leadership whether it be in the home, church, community or your business is showing others how it's done versus telling others how it's done. We have enough of that going on in our government.

Position yourself to be a difference maker. Live with a relentless pursuit of better. Be a leader whose ACTIONS inspire others to do MORE and be MORE. You are destined to be, whatever you decide to be. People always get what they focus on and plan for. So what is our grand master plan?

OUR MASTER PLAN: It's called DOING THINGS!

"Whatever you have learned or received or heard from me, or seen in me, put it into practice." Philippians 4:9

Kevin Mullens

Chapter Four

Battle is the Doorway to Living in the Promise Land

You realize warfare will always exist on this side of eternity when you decide to go to battle within the framework of your mind to defeat negative images of yourself and step out in faith to go live as God promised you. As Dr. Mike Murdock says, "Warfare is always a sign that the enemy has discerned your future." Once you decide to pursue your dreams and live a prosperous life, you will find opposition on every corner. You need not fear because NO WEAPON formed against you shall prosper. Once you start driving the enemy out of your Promised Land you will also understand that the greater the enemy the greater the reward.

God has not only equipped you for the journey but will provide alignment with other believers who have the same mindset. Your faithfulness and loyalty to God's Word will provide light in the darkest of hours and tremendous victory. **"The eyes of the Lord run to and fro throughout the whole earth to SHOW HIMSELF STRONG on behalf of those whose heart is loyal to Him."** 2 Chronicles 16:9

There will always be a battle to fight. The enemy will confront you consistently at where you are presently because he full well knows what you're capable of if you choose to believe what God believes about you. The children of Israel remain a perfect example of how so many people choose to live. Maybe you feel like you have been living in survival mode earning slave wages, overworked and highly underpaid. You know you are a joint-heir to unlimited resources, but you feel like you have no way of accessing the wisdom and wealth in store for you.

"And the LORD said, I have surely seen the affliction of my people which *are* in

Egypt, and have heard their cry by reason of their taskmasters; for I know their sorrows; And I am come down to deliver them out of the hand of the Egyptians, and to bring them up out of that land unto a good land and a large, unto a land flowing with milk and honey; unto the place of the Canaanites, and the Hittites, and the Amorites, and the Perizzites, and the Hivites, and the Jebusites. Now therefore, behold, the cry of the children of Israel is come unto me: and I have also seen the oppression wherewith the Egyptians oppress them." Exodus 3:7-10

I pray that you understand how thoughtful your heavenly Father is. He heard their cry. Brother Branham would say, "The baby that cries the loudest, gets the best service." So, if you are in a current situation and someone offers you a way out, it is possible that you might say, okay whatever you want or even reject the offered help, but when you are sick and tired of your situation and you feel there is no way out, you begin to CRY out to God for deliverance. He responds to that cry the same way a mother would a crying baby.

Now, let us consider that the children of Israel had been in bondage for 400 years. Many of these were born into slavery and from day one only knew torment, whippings, lashings, horrible food and shelter, and such abuse that one would be mentally and physically forced into thinking they were born to live in poverty and shame. There were some that knew of the promise and how God would deliver them, but many had succumbed to the idea that freedom would never exist.

Have you ever heard of Pike Syndrome? I grew up fishing with my dad in small ponds, and my dad would kill any Pike he caught. He knew they were such vicious predators and that one pike could literally eat everything in a small pond. A professor recently did a behavioral study and placed minnows in a tank with a pike and within seconds this carnivorous fish devoured all of the minnows. The professor then placed a glass cylinder in the tank and placed the minnows inside this separate tube. The pike continually smashed into the glass tube attempting to eat the minnows, but every attempt weakened his desire to devour the minnows. Once the pike stopped moving, the professor lifted the glass tube to allow the minnows to co-exist with the pike in the same waters, and the Pike did absolutely nothing. Why? It had convinced itself that the environment had not changed. It was definitely stuck in the past letting recent circumstances dictate its next actions. The pike literally lost all will to live and starved to death although there was an abundance of food.

It's amazing how often we are surrounded with answers to our prayers but because of previous barriers that stood in our way we remain fearful and miss multiple opportunities. As you move from Egypt towards your personal Promised Land, you will have to remove false assumptions and limitations to experience the abundance God has laid up for you.

God raised up a deliverer called Moses who represented salvation to the children of Israel, and through his ministry, provided a supernatural Exodus that was designed to bring them out of bondage and lead them into the Promised Land. The battle for freedom started with accepting God's provided way. No battle was required, YET. But because so many of them were still enslaved in their thinking that even after they walked through the Red Sea and saw the mighty hand of Jehovah work miracles on their behalf, most of them still thought with a bondage, poverty mentality. Just 3 days after being delivered, they begin to murmur and complain about their circumstances. COMPLAINING WEAKENS FAITH! Paul wrote in Philippians 2:14 "...**do everything without complaining and arguing.**" Then Paul often wrote about this journey that took 40 years even though it was a 3 to 5 day journey. Paul said in 1 Corinthians 10:10 (GWT)**, "Don't complain as some of them did. The Angel of death destroyed them.**" Complaining always creates a negative energy that stops the Favor of God from flooding your life with His many blessings. It also represents an ungrateful nature. It's sad how many people today never see the blessings of God because they remain ungrateful. We are told one day perilous times will come when men will be blasphemers, trucebreakers, high-minded, lovers of their own selves and unthankful/ungrateful (2 Timothy 3:1-2). Stop whining and complaining;

Complaining always creates a negative energy that stops the Favor of God.

start embracing the hardship, crisis, and struggle as a chance to reveal your character. The trial isn't meant to defeat you. The journey isn't meant to discourage you but rather to develop you. The only way the children of Israel were ever going to possess the enemy's gates and rightfully live in a prosperous land was to fight. Yes, it's promised to you BUT you are going to have to fight for every inch. Could God had went into the Land of Canaan and wiped out the enemy on their behalf? Yes, but that's not His way of doing things. You are going to have to prepare for battle. As Dr. Mike Murdock says, "David would not have been King had Goliath not existed." The battle was the doorway to the throne. Just because you gave your heart to the Lord doesn't mean you are absent of struggle or battle. You will always be in a fight if you are growing and pursuing what you've been promised, but God has already given you a spirit of victory. God has given you a sword to cut down every enemy and the courage to stand.

"The willingness to fight is the proof you've decided where you belong." Dr. Jerry Grillo, Jr.

I deal with large groups of people on daily basis in my network marketing business, and every day I deal with someone wanting to quit or make excuses or complain about the journey. I cannot encourage you enough to recognize the value of the temporary defeats and setbacks. The greatest of all leaders are the ones who have failed and chose to learn something instead of quit. This adversity will not break you. It is a season that will produce increase if handled correctly.. Your ability to press on and realize that you shall reap in due season if you faint not, is what qualifies you for wealth. It gives you the wisdom to mentor others and offer sound advice when they are in the heat of battle and think there's no victory in sight. You are now their quickest way out of crisis because you have been where they are. Moses had to take them on a desert experience to remove the poverty and slave mindset and prepare them to think like Kings and Queens. Their buzzard mentality was not ready for an eagle experience. They failed to find the wisdom that could be taught while only in the wilderness. They were born rich. They were potentially very wealthy because they were the expressed thoughts of almighty God and the promised seed of Abraham, but until they recognized their position of authority they would continue to think and live like beggars.

"When the LORD thy God shall bring thee into the land whither thou goest to possess it, and hath cast out many nations before thee, the Hittites, and the Girgashites, and the Amorites, and the Canaanites, and the Perizzites, and the Hivites, and the Jebusites, seven nations greater and mightier than thou; <u>And when the LORD thy God shall deliver them before thee; thou shalt smite them, and utterly destroy them; thou shalt make no covenant with them, nor shew mercy unto them:</u> Neither shalt thou make marriages with them; thy daughter thou shalt not give unto his son, nor his daughter shalt thou take unto thy son. For they will turn away thy son from following me, that they may serve other gods: so will the anger of the LORD be kindled against you, and destroy thee suddenly. But thus shall ye deal with them; ye shall destroy their altars, and break down their images, and cut down their groves, and burn their

graven images with fire. For thou *art* an holy people unto the LORD thy God: the LORD thy God hath chosen thee to be a special people unto himself, above all people that *are* upon the face of the earth." Deuteronomy 7:1-6

Imagine all of the years spent in the desert, seeing God's miracles, from a rock that followed them to bring forth water, to being fed supernaturally. You are learning from God's chosen mouthpiece and inwardly longing to finally make it to this land that was promised to you. Then you hear that the land is just a few miles away, and you will soon be living in a land flowing with milk and honey. Then all of a sudden you understand that that are nations living in the land that belongs to you, and they are mightier than you.

So many times the believer thinks that just because he's born again that he is free from battle. The Promised Land never represented the millennium, but it represented the Christian walk. Life here will always be filled with a battle. You cannot advance and enlarge your territory without resistance. When you win the battle within your mind, you are capable of anything. Notice how firm God was on not compromising with the enemy. They were commissioned to destroy the enemy, and to conquer anything taking up residence in a place that did not belong to them. How often do we allow the voice of doubt and our past to haunt us on a daily basis, instead of just destroying it? You can't make a treaty or coexist with negativity. Tearing down cobwebs isn't the answer. You have got to find and destroy the spider if you're going to get rid of the webs that entangle you. You have got to flex your faith muscles and commit to victory in battle if you're going to live in this Promised Land.

In Numbers chapter 13 we find where Moses sent out the 12 spies to go see if the land was all that is was promised to be. Upon arrival each and every spy partook and experienced the vast wealth that was in this land. They came back and reported to Moses, *"Yes Moses, it flows with milk and honey. One cluster of grapes had to be carried by 2 men. It is everything you said it would be, BUT the people in the land are stronger and mightier than us and their cities are fortified. There is no way we can defeat this mighty people for they are giants and **we are but GRASSHOPPERS** in our on sight and in theirs."*

"And there we saw the giants, the sons of Anak, which come of the giants: and we were in our own sight as grasshoppers, and so we were in their sight." Numbers 13:33

We could write an entire book just on this one scripture. It's so important that you realize that however you see yourself is also how others see you. I have traveled literally around the world over the past seven years empowering people to live life unlimited. I realized in the beginning stages of my journey I taught people how to invite, close, communicate effectively and create a winning culture, but all of the skills I taught were rarely put to work by those who come to learn. I mean they cheered. We took pictures together. Many cried and often altar calls were given and business meeting turned to church. However, I would see these same people six months later and they would be at the same place financially or same level in their business that they were when I first taught them.

I quickly realized that many will say, "Yes, I want to be successful," and, "Yes, I'll go do this in a big way," but subconsciously they self-sabotage because they still inwardly battle with self-image issues. Maybe a sense of worthlessness, self-doubt, poverty mindset or negative beliefs that are warring against their conscious state that says, "I want to change."

Most of my messages I send out today to those I mentor are rarely about how to build the business and more on how to build YOU. If we expand your capacity on a subconscious level with positive images, messages, and scriptural confirmation, then everything begins to line up and you become a magnet for success. Your actions will change once your belief system changes about yourself. When you believe you're worthy and deserving of God's blessings both spiritually and naturally then abundance begins to pursue you. When you change, everything changes. When you become more, then you'll earn more. So I continue to help elevate the inner man to dominate your thoughts on a subconscious level so your conscious self acts accordingly. So constantly spend valuable time developing YOU through books, seminars, revival, and correct mentorship because everything you've learned will fall into place and produce amazing results; once YOU get YOU believing that you're a rightful heir to all of

God's promises and whatsoever you desire while praying and believing, that you can have. (Mark 11:24).

10 of the 12 spies brought back a similar report as Joshua and Caleb insomuch that the land was good and plenty. The difference was their attitude and self-image. They were looking through carnal eyes instead of through faith. Your personal perception determines the outcome before anything ever starts. I wish I could just snap my fingers and you would see yourself as your Creator sees you. Everyone is the product of someone's teaching. Parents, professors and friends all have shaped our thoughts and beliefs, whether it is how we vote or raise kids, the types of music we like, the teams we pull for, and definitely, how we view money. The problem occurs when we settle into a life that has been shaped and designed by others. The ten spies were convinced that there would be no way they could drive out the enemy that was living in what was rightfully theirs so the easy thing to do was just retreat. Sadly, when we live a small life we don't serve God or ourselves any justice. We end up influencing those around us to play safe, play small and just accept things as they are. An entire nation chose to believe the report of

these ten spies, and the anger of God was poured out upon them. A generation wandered around in the wilderness for forty years until all were dead. God called their deeds evil because they discouraged the hearts of Israel from possessing what had been promised to them. When Paul writes about this in the book of Hebrews he states that the reason they did not enter that Promised Land was because of UNBELIEF. Everything hinges on your Faith.

Brother Branham said while preaching the Hebrews series in 1957, "But, however, you see, it just goes to show that people don't pay attention to what you're saying. See? Certainly. If I prayed for a person, and I—I tell them people they're going to live. I believe they're going to live. But, no matter, **if my word was absolutely THUS SAITH THE LORD, and you would disbelieve it, you'd die**, anyhow. Certainly. Here is THUS SAITH THE LORD, and many of them receive it and die. Many of them go to hell, when, THUS SAITH THE LORD, 'You don't have to.' Is that right? [Congregation says, "Amen."—Ed.] Sure. See? It's what… **It's all based on your faith."**

Just as Faith can move mountains, unbelief stops the favor of God. Even Jesus said He was in a place where He could not do many mighty works because of THEIR unbelief; but just as there are masses who choose to be controlled by fear or the appearance of the circumstance, there are also elite warriors of faith that understand that whatsoever things they desire when they pray, and BELIEVE that they shall receive them… they shall have them. Joshua and Caleb represented such faith.

"And Caleb stilled the people before Moses, and said, Let us go up at once, and possess it; for we are well able to overcome it." Numbers 13:30

Oh, I can feel the spirit of almighty God begin to swell up within me when I think of the boldness and authority Joshua and Caleb spoke with. They said, "DO NOT FEAR the people of the land for they are bread for us." They had a different spirit within them. The people were crying, complaining and begging to go back to slavery in Egypt while just over the river was the land that was rightfully theirs.

I plead with you to have the spirit of Joshua and Caleb. Embrace the promises of God by believing them with unwavering faith and great expectation. I want you to experience the pressed down, shaken, running over nature of God's many blessings rather than reciting scriptures your entire life but never seeing them manifested due to unbelief. That spirit lingers and grabs a hold of your kids and their kids and creates a generational curse.

Joshua and Caleb were two out of two and a half million that entered into the Promised Land. Although a stubborn, rebellious, disbelieving generation died in the wilderness; children were born in the desert that never knew slavery, so their minds were free to embrace the will of God in their lives. They were believers in the same faith that drove Joshua and Caleb to go forth and take the land. They had some fight in them. They never suffered with a grasshopper mentality but were strong in faith to believe ALL God had promised them. Joshua reached a place where he challenged their faith and willingness to confront and defeat the enemy. Joshua said, **"How long will you be SLACK to go in and possess the land which the Lord, the God of your fathers, HAS GIVEN YOU (Joshua 18:3)?"** You will never possess anything that you are unwilling to pursue. The level of your pursuit reveals your true heart's desire. Are you a slacker? Someone who moves slowly, lacking in activity? Oh how the enemy loves to keep us in motion but not taking action. Running in circles like the children of Israel did when the whole time they were days from living in the Promise.

"Laziness moves so slow that poverty eventually overtakes it." Benjamin Franklin

You have got to figure out if what you are doing is getting you closer to where you want to be. There will always be giants standing in your way and possessing your desired home, land, or potential income. It's yours, if you'll fight for it. Fight for every inch knowing God promised you that when the enemy comes in like a flood the spirit of the Lord will lift up a standard on your behalf (Isaiah 59:19). Do not think or dream small again. Your enemy fears your future so he will bring warfare and distraction to keep you believing the evil report that you aren't worthy, much less capable. But believe the report of the Lord.

Your weapon of choice... DELIBERATE ACTION.

You are designed and created to flow in the

abundant. Your family, health, finances, self-image, and spiritual walk - just to name a few - all have a capacity for more. Let that same spirit that charged Joshua and Caleb to say, "We are well able to overcome," abide in you. Do not accept substitutions any longer. You have big things to do and many are waiting on you to show up and help lead them to freedom. Your weapon of choice... DELIBERATE ACTION. When you take deliberate action, things begin to happen. You literally annihilate fear and all forms of procrastination. DON'T YOU DARE SETTLE FOR LESS THAN GOD HAS PROMISED YOU!!!

"May our barns be filled with crops of every kind. May the flocks in our fields multiply by the thousands, even tens of thousands, and may our oxen be loaded down with produce. May there be no enemy breaking through our walls, no going into captivity, no cries of alarm in our town squares. Yes, joyful are those who live like this! Joyful indeed are those whose God is the LORD." Psalms 144:13-15

The trials you face are there to prove your faith, to bring you forth as pure gold that's been tried in the fire. Do not despise these moments, because they are needed to forge and reveal character. Many will say, I want to leave Egypt and all will say, I would love to live in the Promised Land, but few will ever be willing to face the giants. As the old hymn says, "Some through the waters, some through the flood, some through deep trials, but all through the blood." You are redeemed, justified and truly ordained to charge the gates of the enemy and possess what was promised to you.

"Don't wish it was easier, wish you were better. Don't wish for less problems, wish for more skills. Don't wish for less challenges, wish for more wisdom." Jim Rohn

Chapter Five

The Wisdom of Ants

"Go to the ant, you sluggard; consider its ways and be wise! It has no commander, no overseer or ruler, yet it stores its provisions in summer and gathers its food at harvest. How long will you lie there, you sluggard? When will you get up from your sleep? A little sleep, a little slumber, a little folding of the hands to rest - and poverty will come on you like a thief and scarcity like an armed man." Proverbs 6:6-11

The ant is a perfect example for us to draw wisdom from as we consider what's required of us to see goals and plans fulfilled. As you choose to expect more out of life, it would do you a great service to not only study the wisdom of the ant but lives of men and women who have beat the odds. Stories of people that help you gather the information needed to develop your skills and faith in a better future. The ant is focused. FOCUS is the super power of the highly successful and wealthy. They fully understand that you will draw towards you and ultimately manifest whatever your dominant thoughts are. The ant is programmed to prepare and finish its task; very goal oriented but charged with a burning desire to finish what it has started. When its summer, the ant is thinking winter. They are master investors as they are always laying up treasures in the storehouse. So many people today are unprepared for any future at all. They are sluggards as it relates to knowing what to do but always finding excuses to do nothing. Most people today don't even have a savings account. If they went a week or two without work they'd fall behind on their bills or potentially lose something to the bank.

I meet many as I'm building teams of people internationally that are on the verge of retirement and are broke. They have either bought in to the idea that the government is going to take care of them or hoping their kids will. The Bible says a good man leaves an inheritance for his kids, kids (Proverbs 13:22). More scriptural teaching on our responsibility to lay up for oncoming generations. Teach your kids to invest now, no matter how low the return on investment; so when wintertime comes they will have prepared for the storm. Find a successful trusted advisor or investor to help turn your money into more money. Rich people plan for three generations to come while poor people plan for Saturday night. You will never have a life of complete happiness if you continue to do just enough to get by. Start gathering ideas and strategies for your plan, but you have to start executing your plan. There is no time to waste. Absorb all of the information you can so that you acquire the right mindset, skill and connections to accelerate success in every area of your life.

Notice that the ant is very small and not very strong but doesn't have a self-image issue. We all have a choice. There is one infallible and very powerful key that you must possess if you are going to conquer your fears and live life as you truly desire and that is a Positive Attitude. Thomas Jefferson: **"Nothing can stop the man with the right mental attitude from achieving his goal; nothing on earth can help the man with the**

wrong mental attitude." I love how Brother Branham placed this same approach on seeing God's promises fulfilled in your life when he said, "The right mental attitude towards any promise of God will bring it to pass." It's not enough to just read God's Word if you are not going to believe the promises are applicable for your day and your life. Stop making God's Word a history book. His Word does not go forth and come back void (Isaiah 55:11). What He declares, He will also bring to pass. Stop struggling with your inner self. If you don't commit to a winning attitude then your attempts will always fall short, and you will self-sabotage or simply quit. The ant - like a lot of us - is small. If you are not small in stature, you might be small and feel insignificant within. We know that as a man thinks in his heart, so is he (Proverbs 23:7). The Apostle Paul spent years in prison and upon release to stand before King Agrippa he was asked if he had anything to say. Paul's first words were, 'I THINK MYSELF HAPPY." He refused to allow his circumstances to determine his choices or affect his inner man which controlled the outer man. Maybe he had read where King David was very distressed one time because the people spoke of stoning him to death and the scripture said, "David encouraged himself" (I Samuel 30:6). Can't you see how valuable the right mental attitude is? Your belief in who you are creates an environment that tells the entire world who you are.

The ant does not quit. 2 Chronicles 15:7 **"But as for you, be strong and DO NOT GIVE UP, for your work will be rewarded."** So much can be said for the attitude of getting things done. Calvin Coolidge once said, "Persistence and determination are omnipotent." The ant has a motor that never turns off. As a kid, I would pour water on ant piles thinking I was getting rid of these pesky ants by destroying their habitat. The next morning the ant pile would be back again like nothing ever happened. I would place objects in front of ants that were harvesting food, thinking I'd get them to move on someplace else. They were unshaken by my feeble attempts to stop them, because they were determined to find a way no matter what. That mental toughness and superior focus is what's needed today rather we are trying to change our own circumstances or the local communities we live in. Start asking yourself how often do you start something but quit. How easily are you distracted after setting a goal? How fast do you tap out when life has you pinned down? What's the difference between those who never reach their goals, year after year, and those who achieve one goal after another, and it often seems like everything they touch turns to gold? It's generally because they are self-driven and self-motivated. Self-motivation is the force that keeps pushing us to go on even though it doesn't seem possible. It's our internal drive to achieve, produce, develop, and keep moving forward. When you think you're ready to quit something, or you just don't know how to start, your self-motivation is what pushes you to go on.

Can I tell you that there is a warrior living within you that wants to fight through the fears that paralyze you from moving forward? I can remember reading an African proverb that says, "Every morning in Africa, a gazelle wakes up, it knows it must outrun the fastest lion or it will be killed. Every morning in Africa, a lion wakes up. It knows it must run faster than the slowest gazelle, or it will starve. It doesn't matter whether you're the lion or a gazelle—when the sun comes up, you'd better be running." This parable lends credit to the harsh reality of life and how it can be full of stress and competition. But it also provides a wakeup call for those who want a life of meaningful purpose. God will help those that help themselves. You're not here to just survive. I want you to recognize that the Lion of the tribe of Judah lives within you, and you were predestinated to be the head and not the tail (Deut. 28). Life won't give you what you want, but it will give you what you accept. Don't let the jungle beat you down and starve you out of your glorious inheritance. Run; don't walk in the pursuit of living an abundant life. You were ordained to be blessed so you can be a blessing. The enemy of mediocrity will not go away easily, but once you feed the faith within and stop being the victim, you will become the victor. Get rid of the notion that you're the subject of bad luck or that you're just playing the hand you were dealt. You will always be the victim of whatever you tolerate; whether it is an abusive relationship, addiction or financial misery. You will never eliminate the problem by tolerating it. Earl Nightingale put it best when he said, "People are where they are because that is exactly where they really want to be – whether they will admit it or not." The children of Israel had to destroy the enemy in order to live in the Promised Land. The greatest enemy we will ever face is ourselves. You have been given a choice to live or die, be blessed or cursed. And God said, "CHOOSE LIFE." The choice itself requires action. Can't you see more clearly how important is to JUST DO IT?

The ant has a support group and works in unity with others that help bare the load and offer help. Separate yourself from people who do not support your dreams. If you hang around 4 broke people, you will be the fifth. If you hang around 4 millionaires, you will be the fifth. Show me your friends, and I'll show you your future. You were born an eagle so you don't **Change your conversation and you will change your destiny.** belong down in the barnyard roosting with chickens. Friends create conversation, and your future is attached to your conversation. Change your conversation, and you will change your destiny. You will never be able to hold an eagle conversation with someone who has a buzzard's mentality. Surround yourself with people that push you to get out of your comfort zone and experience life so you can be all that God has called you to be.

Notice how the wisdom of the ant indicts the

sluggard for his sleep. A little sleep, a little folding of the hands and BOOM, POVERTY comes upon you like a thief. How long will you lie there asks the ant? We should be full aware by now that God wants you to be rich. Yes, I said it! His own plan for you is that you'd prosper (Jeremiah 29:11). He takes pleasure when His servants prosper (Psalms 35:27). He feels those that love Him with treasuries and gives them wealth (Proverbs 8:32). He declares that His blessings will make you rich, and He will add no sorrow to it (Proverbs 10:22). What an incredible Father that wishes ABOVE ALL THINGS that you would prosper (3 John 1:2). You were empowered to prosper (Deuteronomy 8:18). Do not struggle with accepting God's desire for you to sow seed and see an abundant increase. Jesus taught on money 5 times more than he did prayer. There are 500 scriptures where He taught on prayer and 2,000 where He taught on income. Stop wondering if God desires for you to have wealth. The wisdom in wealth is having the right mindset and heart so you can master money and use it as a tool to advance the Kingdom. David wrote in Psalm chapter 1 that those that delight in the Law of God will prosper in whatever he does. We need men and women of

God in our local and global marketplace that have created significant income, so that our voice will have more authority and influence. **"For the LORD your God will bless you as He has promised you, and you will lend to many nations, but you will not borrow; and you will rule over many nations, but they will not rule over you"** - Deuteronomy 15:6.

Now that gets me excited. You don't have to be in debt and be a servant to the lender but apply kingdom principles in the right places of business and become the lender. God has unlimited resources and lack of money is obviously not an issue to him. As joint heirs of His economy lets take notice from the ant that now is the time to take deliberate action. We have too much to do and we have sit by too long waiting on things to happen instead of designing a life and making things happen.

"And don't never be afraid to ask big things. **God wants you to ask big things. He don't want you to be little petty and juvenile. He wants you to ask big things that your joys may be full. Could you imagine a little fish about that big, way**

out yonder in the Atlantic Ocean, say, 'I better drink just a little bit of this water, I might run out.' Nonsense. Could you imagine a little mouse about that big down there in the great garners of Egypt, saying, 'I just better eat two grains a day, 'cause I might run out before summertime again.' Well, that's nonsense. If they had ten hundred thousand rats that size, they'd never eat it up. And they had billions times billions of tons of them fish, they'd never drink the water up. And how many times could we multiply; you could never exhaust God in His powers and His mercies to His children. <u>He's the inexhaustible Fountain of Life. Just drink, and drink, and drink, and drink.</u>" 56-1215 - Hear Ye Him, Brother Branham.

Now that we know the endless possibilities, it's up to us to do something with our passion and dreams. When you add action to your dreams it becomes oxygen to the soul. On my team of world changers I am privileged to mentor and be in covenant with people that have conquered their past or overcome identity crisis to create wealth for their families. Many who were battling self-doubt or in debt or lost without direction are today making more in a month than most make in a year. HOW? They begin to read the right books, and pursue learning with a passion. They joined my network marketing team at the same level everyone else did, with access to the same products and compensation as everyone else did. So what separates these top income earners and over achievers? It's not their college degrees, ability to speak or overall great DNA. They simply learned the business by doing the business and through staying tied in to successful leadership they quickly figured out that others may be more talented but there was no reason for anyone to ever outwork them. The harder they work, the luckier they get! Ask yourself, are you qualified to sleep? Solomon said, "Love not sleep, lest thou come to poverty" (Proverbs 20:13). Of course it was Solomon that taught us to seek wisdom and to be diligent and persistent. Society will call us dreamers, but we are the ones who don't sleep. There is a great quote on this subject by Eric Thomas that says, "Sleep is the new broke. If you only have 24 hours in a day, your success is dependent upon how you spend the 24." Let others live small and ordinary lives but not you. Let others allow the opinions of others to determine their destiny, but not you. While others are working on their tan, or spending hours in front of the TV, or playing X-box all night, you are going the extra mile doing the things day in and day out to secure your families future. You have chosen to succeed on purpose. You will feel exhausted and often will want to quit, but hear the champion within telling you that you can make it. You were ordained for this. Your WHY is now bigger than your WHY NOT. Let the Wisdom of the Ant keep you on track and remind you of the great rewards that await those that are persistent and don't quit and the consequences of distraction, complacency and laziness. It is far easier to create wealth and financial freedom than one might think. It all starts with YOU.

"It had long since come to my attention that people of accomplishment rarely sat back and let things happen to them. They went out and happened to things." Leonardo Da Vinci

The Dream Stealers seek to hijack your destiny by sabotaging your life at your mental, physical, spiritual and financial levels, with the intent of getting you to stand still rather than take action. Anything they can do to get you feeling lost with no direction or purpose. Their objective is to render you powerless in every area of your life so you never access your blessing. Their only agenda is to poison your mind with thoughts of unbelief and confusion. The giants had hijacked the Children of Israel's destiny by stealing their land and claiming it as theirs. The devil is a thief and will rob you of living as God promised if you coward down and walk away. Gain wisdom from the ant. The ant refuses to allow poverty to exist. It invests in its future through targeted activity, and its work ethic is unparalleled. Though small and often overlooked its inner divine self is driven by an unwavering faith to conquer anything in its path and stay on course. It knows no limits and is constantly expanding its territory. The ants' secret to success? Be relentless every day, all day and don't quit, don't ever quit. Find a way or make a way, but don't ever quit. Colonel Sanders, who is world famous today, would've never had his story of triumph told had he quit. Did you know that he was retired and broke when he decided enough was enough and set out to sell his fried chicken recipe? No after no, rejection was mounting up and he was often sleeping in his car, but his internal compass kept him heading towards his desired goal. After being told no 1,009 times something amazing happened. He finally got a yes!!! Colonel Sanders become a multi-millionaire through taking massive deliberate action and having the determination to NEVER QUIT on his dream. Don't let your dream fade away until it no longer haunts you at night. If you are waiting on the right time or skillset or the right connections, then prosperity will never find you. The ant knew prosperity finds those that are found tirelessly pursuing and working towards their dreams. If you quit: you don't deserve it, so get back in the game of life and succeed on purpose.

Kevin Mullens

Chapter Six

Great Things Come to Those Who ~~WAIT~~, TAKE ACTION

Although there is great wisdom to be found in patience, this old saying - like many - do not hold true when talking about finishing a goal or succeeding in life or business. We could say that those who wait will only get what's left behind from those that hustle and make things happen. Now that you have given yourself permission to be successful, the time is NOW for you to unleash your full potential. Allow your dreams and deepest desires to consume your thoughts as you take decisive action to achieve them. It will not be easy. Paul Orberson used to say, "Enemy thought number one is this it is going to be easy." It's always a struggle to develop a new mindset and get rid of self-limiting doubts and bad habits, but a little push in the right direction every single day will launch your life into extreme momentum. No amount of thinking and reading positive self-help books has gotten you any closer to where you want to be. It's not what you say that matters but what you do - day in and day out - with a never give up attitude that'll make the difference. Can you imagine where we'd be today had Thomas Edison never acted upon his ideas? The thing that will separate you from everyone else is to make up your mind to go for it and have no plan to retreat. Don't be afraid to fail or be laughed at because one day they will copy you. You can't radically alter your life from a passive position, and you won't win the game of wealth until you TAKE ACTION.

Frederick Douglass was born in 1818 as a slave, but Frederick was never a slave in his mind. His life would become a witness for all that no one has a right to determine your worth or control your destiny but YOU. Frederick was one of the most revered abolitionists as he dazzled audiences with his ability to speak and was a constant advocate for equality for everyone. He stated that, "knowledge was the pathway from slavery to freedom." Of course, believers know that people are even destroyed today for a lack of knowledge. Not education! The world is full of people with degrees that are as useless as the paper they're written on Knowledge and wisdom are altogether different things, and they are available to anyone. Wisdom is what you learn from life's lessons or through mentorship, which can be wisdom without pain (Dr. Mike Murdock). In the early years, Douglass was repeatedly beaten in an attempt to break him physiologically, but Frederick would not break. It's so true that most men have wishes but few have WILL POWER. I love to read the inspirational stories of people who were faced with being disabled due to tragic circumstances or confronted with death and instead of letting the situation define them; they decided to define the situation. Will Power is the ability to bring everything under your authority and not give in. Frederick was a firm believer in God's Word, and it was his source of inspiration as he continued to be a leader in the anti-slavery movement. He had a strong conviction to forgive in spite of what he had gone through and believed that everyone needed to be converted.

We have a lot of preachers, telling everyone

what needs to be done without actually doing anything at all. We are supposed to be doers of the word, not just hearers (James 1:22). I know I have been guilty a time or two of this in my life. I meet people every day that has read the book, "Think and Grow Rich" or even the Bible from cover to cover, but the words never take root in their life and bring forth ACTION. Frederick continued to break down barriers by becoming a bestselling author and also working with President Lincoln, Johnson and Grant. He was the first African American nominated for Vice President in 1872. His accolades are too many to mention, and his legacy will be forever remembered. However, Frederick's story would've never been told had he waited around on someone else to stand up and fight.

I meet so many people who do not like the elected politicians or the way government operates, but these same people are often guilty of never voting themselves. The world is full of people that love to complain about the way things are but never do anything about it. Never get involved. Although Frederick might have suffered the pain of natural slavery, he found the courage to escape and make a difference so others might experience freedom as well. Many today are operating as if they have no choice. You live in a society where information is readily available. You have access to anything you want if you will apply yourself and be persistent. Today the MLM industry is a 200 Billion Dollar industry that is growing at a rapid pace, and no one needs a fancy resume to get started. A place where you can earn what you believe your worth based on what you're willing to. No one is making you remain an employee where you help build and create other peoples' wealth while you earn a wage. No one has a legitimate excuse any longer on staying where they are. Frederick spent his entire life making a difference. His passion was the fuel that ignited his actions, and his actions created a movement that changed history.

"I prayed for freedom for twenty years, but received no answer until I prayed with my legs." Frederick Douglass

Too many Christians are guilty of praying, but treating God like He's a magical lamp that just grants requests without anything being required. . Scripture says that God is a Rewarder of those that diligently seek Him (Hebrews 11:6). Even God's reward system requires persistence. He loves to Favor those that thirst after Him. Are you diligent in getting what you want? The critical point where many fail is in waiting around on God to make you healthier or grow your bank account without action from you. Could He? Yes. For instance, God said He gives you the power to get wealth but the word power in this scripture means ability. In every scripture that has abundance attached to it there is something required of you. Frederick finally woke up and realized God was not ignoring his prayer but waiting on him to take action. Remember Noah had to build the Ark. Joshua had to drive out the enemy to possess the Promised Land. I pray you will rise up when you hear God saying, "Whom shall I send?" and say, "Here I am Lord, SEND ME!" Your prayer without action is powerless.

You must remember that you are creating a culture and that culture in your home or business is a direct reflection of you. So be mindful of where you place the most focus and always remember that changing any culture requires action from you. People don't do what you say, they do what you do! One preacher said, "If you want your people to bleed than you've got to hemorrhage." Lay it all on the line. Your success in both your spiritual and natural life is hidden in your daily routine. Pray with your legs not just your lips.

Many times God responds to our prayers by equipping and empowering us to be the very answers to our prayers. Too many times we are also guilty of praying about things God has already called or commissioned us to do. You can ask God to grow your church, but you've got to go witness in the local community. You can ask God to help you grow your business, but you have got to sow seed. In network marketing, it's common for people to feel stuck or even going backwards. My mentor Paul Orberson would say, "You should get up every day and ask yourself one question. If my downline did what I did today then how big would my check be?" Wow! So much wisdom packed into that statement but yet so simple. We are responsible for our beliefs, for our actions and ultimately for our own success.

You must visualize and imagine how it will feel living in your dream home, boarding your private jet to spend a weekend in Fiji or have the funds necessary to pursue whatever you feel you're called to do without financial restraint. Then your long-term goal must be broken down in much smaller day to day goals that are believable and doable. Let's say you wanted $25,000 liquid cash in the bank in five years. That's a number that would scare most people living paycheck to paycheck, but if you broke it down and saved $5,000 a year over next five years you would have met your goal.

What if you broke down the $25,000 over a week for the five years? You would only need to save $96 a week in order to reach your goal. Of course, you can create a more believable scenario using this method with any goal you set, no matter how big it is. If it's a massive goal than you need to immerse yourself in whatever information or skill connected to that goal so you can be properly prepared. Anybody can, but will you? Will you qualify for wealth, increase or uncommon favor? To qualify for God's abundance there is criteria. Do you serve Him and acknowledge His ways? Do you Tithe and sow into the Kingdom? Do you give generously? Do you apply His principles of wealth in the right

We are responsible for our beliefs, for our actions and ultimately for our success.

places with expectation that the seed produces a harvest that will move you from even to overflow?

"Practice these things, IMMERSE yourself in them, so that all may see your progress" 1 Timothy 4:15. Another version of this scripture says, **"Meditate upon these things; give thyself WHOLLY to them; that thy PROFITING may appear to all"**.

Remember, you will never take perfect action. You are going to be criticized by people who are too lazy to do anything about their dreams. Have you ever seen a hater doing better than you? Me neither! Doing things is difficult because it requires discipline, focus and repetitive action. Yes, you are going to mess up and get it wrong. Every successful person to do anything worthwhile has failed over and over. F-E-A-R either means, Fear Everything And Run or Face Everything And Rise. You have heard me mention *Taking Massive Action* quite a few times. In simple terms, it's just doing a lot of things every day for a long period of time in the direction of your dreams. One more meeting, one more call. Getting up earlier than most and going to bed later than most.

Let others sleep while you hustle and grind. MAXIMUM EFFORT always equals MAXIMUM REWARDS. Action is the bridge between your dreams and living your dreams. You have got to endure and be a finisher. You will master the skills needed to dominate thru repeated behavior and when the shifting begins to occur in your life, you will witness how quickly the world will step aside as opportunities, wealth and favor pursue you. Remember, that you are what you consistently do; not what start doing or do every once in a while but what you consistently do. Go back and review many of your on prayers and goals that seem to have gone unanswered or even forgotten and start praying like Frederick did. He prayed with his legs.

"TELL THE WORLD WHAT YOU INTEND TO DO, BUT FIRST SHOW IT. This is the equivalent of saying "Deeds, and not words, are what count most." You are the master of your destiny. You can influence, direct and control your own environment. You can make your life what you want it to be." — Napoleon Hill

Final Thoughts: Paying the Price

There will be no shortcuts on this road to success. Even Jesus taught that if you were going to build a tower, would you not count the cost first. Of course, Jesus paid the greatest price that we might live. The price is typically too demanding which is why most would rather settle for where they are in life versus paying the price to achieve and live extraordinary. Will it be easy? NO! Will it be worth it? YES! Henry Thoreau said, "The cost of a thing is the amount of life which is required in exchange for it." Church goers too often are the majority in wanting a life that produces much fruit but far too often unwilling to do anything about it. Whether it be the fasting and praying required to walk in a deeper more spiritual place, the amount of studying a successful pastor or minister puts into knowing God's Word so they can effectively preach and be anointed, the amount of things a doctor gives up to become a doctor, or the things an Olympic athlete might put on hold in order to compete at the highest level. Whatever the desire is, it will require sacrifice and tremendous discipline, but the rewards will be life changing.

I'd like to suggest that your hunger and thirst for success be equally matched by your hunger to know God on a more intimate level as well. It seems that when both of these are in harmony that the door to wealth is kicked open wide and it flows like a river. "**Commit your actions to the Lord, and your plans WILL SUCCEED**" (Proverbs 16:3) I want your wealth and increase to come through applying these infallible Kingdom Principles as you begin to take MASSIVE ACTION so you remain humble in your journey. "**By humility and the fear of the LORD are riches, and honour, and life**" (Proverbs 22:4) A lot of poor people consider themselves to be humble, and it's partially because their circumstances have forced them into being humble. But in this journey to live life more

> "Commit your actions to the Lord, and your plans WILL SUCCEED" (Proverbs 16:3)

abundant you have to be humble in accepting that there are better ways to get you where you want to be than the one that you are currently on. Humble yourself to a good mentor who will correct you, guide you and promote you.

Paying the price doesn't mean disregarding integrity or selling your soul to the devil at the crossroads. It's about measuring the amount of pain you will face in order to be a champion. The price is steep, even if you desire to just be a nun or monk, giving up worldly things, in order to serve a higher purpose. The price in time, effort and energy, along with many other forms of currency, is the investment of being great. People often say, "Well I wouldn't want to travel like you do or do what you do," when they see how successful I have been in building teams around the world and generating a 7 figure a year income. . Of course, they won't have what I have either. Look, you can either sign up for life without parole (JOB), have little to nothing at the end of your journey to enjoy retirement or leave an inheritance to your kids, OR you could spend a few years taking deliberate action in a business, real estate, stock or an MLM business and create a source of positive cash flow that would continue to pay you over and over for what you started, not what you do. It's like pushing that huge ball up the mountain. It's hard! It feels impossible and completely exhausting, but once you get that investment or people helping people business to the top of that mountain and it reaches the tipping point. You will have created an unstoppable force that creates such a movement that things all of sudden seem easy.

The true path to success is in serving many. What you make happen for others, God will make happen for you. If you don't learn how to get paid when you sleep, you will work until you die. Success becomes a way of life. You got to stop sowing in another man's field, or you will always get a wage and the owner of the field will always get the profits/harvest.

Jim Rohn actually said it was easier to get rich than to explain not getting rich. Your bank account suffers because you are missing some information that is needed in order to access wealth. Everything you currently are is the result of previous thinking. Many poor people live with a lottery mindset while the wealthy live with an action mindset. Gather the information from someone who has what you want or someone who has been where you're trying to get, and if you DO

WHAT THEY DO, you will GET WHAT THEY`VE GOT.

When you expand your thinking capacity it will increase your earning potential. Leaders are readers. "Poor people have a big TV and rich people have a big library" – Jim Rohn. Do not get lazy on learning. Pursue learning passionately. What will you give up in order to get what you want? You will have to empty out something to make room for something to be poured in. What you are doing now is determining your future.

Give your goals some deadlines. Make sure your goals are written down. They have no chance of being achieved if you do not write them down and give them life. You need something to hold you accountable, and goals with deadlines have a voice. You now have a clear vision or dream on what you want to achieve so the next step is setting a goal. The deadline within your goal will create an adrenaline rush of unusual determination to finish the task to complete the goal. Always have the image of the end result desired held firmly within your mind so you are positioning yourself for success. Accept 100% responsibility for your life. You must have a plan to follow. Life will always be getting in the way of your well laid out plans, so make sure above all things that you take action immediately. ACTION trumps everything else. Constant hoping and wishing will drain your positive energy. Taking action will elevate your energy to produce and be effective. When you fully commit to reading the right books and becoming passionate about learning, you will begin to too create a millionaire mindset through mastering your thoughts. This, of course, becomes the anchor of what we believe, and whatever you believe, you will DO. What is inside of you pushing you?

Many people today have access to everything the super-rich do and often attend their seminars receiving this priceless information. So why is it that for some it works and pays off and for others it doesn't? One word, COMMITMENT! **It is the toll gate on the road to financial freedom that everyone must pass through.** This is by far the critical factor in whether you will pay the price over the long haul to create wealth. Those that are partially committed will study, prepare and consider themselves busy but rarely get results. You got to be in it to win it. Being fully committed is about playing hard and showing up every single day. Distraction is the enemy of prosperity, so committed people eliminate distractions. They embrace risk and adversity. They don't see failure but lessons learned. Their ambition and tenacity on a daily basis creates a compound effect that multiplies their growth exponentially. Your action is literally the byproduct of your commitment. Without commitment the actions needed to succeed will never get done because something else is always getting in the way.

Commitment ignites actions. Without commitment the external world wins the battle for your time causing wealth and financial freedom to forever remain a pipe dream. Financial mediocrity doesn't require much, but the price of admission to creating wealth will be commitment. You don't need to be an expert. An expert, as they say, was once a beginner. Your commitment to anything signifies priority, and whatever you place in high regard will become the thing you pursue the most. The so called secret is a deep commitment to your goals that lasts long enough to surpass your excuses or desires to quit, and effects your actions in such a way that you get results.

"WHEN HE OPENS DOORS, NO ONE WILL BE ABLE TO CLOSE THEM" ISAIAH 22:22

This year will be a year of unanswered prayers being answered. You might even be thinking you've somehow missed God's Favor or have been forgotten. God has seen your faithfulness even in spite of your circumstances. You are going to see the floodgates of almighty God flood your life with blessings you didn't even pray for. Do not be intimidated by your current situation. God said in His Word that you can pray with faith and whatever you desire, you can have. He gave you the ability to overcome. The limitations and restraints that have held you back are NO MORE! It doesn't matter if you think you're not qualified. God doesn't call the qualified, but He qualifies the called. You're worried you don't have the right skills or talent, but all God needs is a surrendered vessel with an unconquered mind and your willingness to take action. He will produce the right resources and people in your life to manifest His purpose in your life. God created you to live an abundant life and when the wind of Favor blows your direction it's unexplainable. There are NO limits to His power. He's the inexhaustible fountain of life. The impossible does not exist in His presence. So prepare your house for success and do not be shaken by the enemy's voice of negativity and doubt. I don't care if you've gotten 1 million no's... All you need is a Yes by Jesus. Today you see things differently and with great expectation you accept the shifting of God's Favor on your behalf!

"YOU CROWN THE YEAR WITH YOUR GOODNESS, AND YOUR PATHS DRIP WITH ABUNDANCE." Psalms 65:11

KEEP
CALM
AND
TAKE
MASSIVE
ACTION